Bear Grylls

SURVIVAL SKILLS HANDBOOK

SUMMER

Bear Grylls

This survival skills handbook was specially put together to help young adventurers like you to stay safe in the wild. Summer is an ideal time to explore the great outdoors. The weather is mostly warm and dry, plants and trees will be blooming, and there will be lots of plants and animals for you to discover. This book will give you all the skills you need to make the most of a summer adventure – so get out there and have fun!

Bear.

CONTENTS

KIT AND CLOTHING

Summer is a great time to get outdoors, whether you go hiking, camping, swimming, boating, or just for a walk around your local area. However, you need to hone your survival skills to stay safe in the wild. Preparation is vital – and that includes taking the right gear.

Clothing

In summer, it's best to wear cotton or a fabric that absorbs sweat. Pack a warm layer in case it gets cool, and always bring wet-weather gear, as you never know when you might get caught in a summer downpour! You'll need sturdy, waterproof boots and a sun hat. Cut-off trousers can transform into shorts. Avoid tight jeans, as they'll restrict your movement and get soaked through if it rains.

Sun protection

The sun's rays are fiercest in summer. Exposed skin can burn in just a few minutes, so cover up or apply sunscreen or sunblock. Wear sunglasses to protect your eyes from sunlight, and never look directly at the sun. Drink plenty of water, as dehydration is a risk in summer heat.

Equipment

These items are important for all summer expeditions.

mobile phone

torch

trail snacks

water bottle

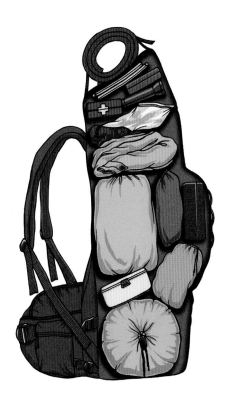

Packing your rucksack

Knowing how to correctly pack your rucksack can save you a lot of time and energy. Pack your rucksack in reverse order, with the things you need first on top, and items, such as your sleeping bag, that you won't need until you reach camp, at the bottom. Put essential kit, such as map and water bottle, in side-pockets where you can lay hands on them easily. If there is a chance of rain, pack your things in plastic bags to keep them dry. Some rucksacks come with a built-in waterproof liner.

✖ BEAR SAYS

Your rucksack should have a hip belt to take the weight off your shoulders. Adjust straps for maximum comfort.

WEATHER WATCHING

Summer weather is generally pleasant, but be careful, because it can be changeable. A clear blue sky can quickly turn cloudy, bringing with it a risk of rain and thunderstorms. Stay alert for hazards such as wind, mist, and fog.

How thunderstorms form

In hot, sticky weather, warm, moist air rises to form tall, dark cumulonimbus clouds. The tops of these clouds develop a positive electric charge (shown on the diagram as a red +), while the base becomes negatively charged (shown as a blue −). When the charge is great enough, lightning sparks between clouds, or from clouds to the ground.

Sheltering in a storm

Don't shelter on an exposed ridge or under a lone tree, as these places can attract lightning. If you're swimming, leave the water immediately. You'll be safer in a car, valley, wood, or in a ditch or gully. If possible, try to get indoors. If caught in the open, discard metal objects such as walking poles and umbrellas. Crouch down and raise your arms to protect your head.

How far away?

You can work out how far away a storm is by counting the seconds between the lightning flash and thunderclap. Sound takes three seconds to travel a kilometre, so divide the number of seconds by three.

Mountain weather

Mountains have a much colder climate than lowland areas, even in summer. The weather up there changes fast, and can get worse in just a few minutes. Prepare for cold, windy conditions on summits and wear several layers of clothing.

Mist and fog

These hazards are caused by low-level cloud. In thick fog, it's very hard to get your bearings. You will need a map and compass to find your way (see pages 12–15).

BEAR SAYS

Always check the forecast before setting out on an expedition. Be aware of changing conditions, such as gathering clouds and rising winds.

Weather maps

Learning to read weather maps will be invaluable on a summer expedition, with risk of fast-changing weather. These maps use symbols to show sunshine, clouds, rain, and also wind speeds and direction. Lines called isobars link places with the same air pressure. When isobars are close together, it will likely be wet and windy.

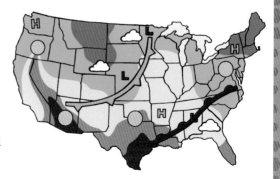

HOT WEATHER HEALTH

You need to be careful in hot weather, as there are several risks to your health. The body's natural cooling system can fail, bringing about heatstroke, and direct sunlight can badly burn unprotected skin. Take action to avoid these hazards of summer weather.

Heat exhaustion

Heat exhaustion is caused by excessive sweating in hot, humid conditions. The skin feels clammy, and you may feel weak, dizzy, or even delirious. If you feel this coming on, rest in the shade and drink water with a pinch of salt to replace lost fluids.

Heatstroke

Also called sunstroke, this is the most serious form of heat exhaustion and can be fatal if left untreated. Symptoms include high temperature, fast pulse, headaches, dizziness, nausea, and vomiting. Rest in the shade under a damp sheet or with a fan to cool down, and drink cool water or juice.

Sunburn

A bad sunburn can blister the skin and, in extreme cases, lead to skin cancer. Prevent sunburn by covering your skin or applying sunscreen. To treat sunburn, protect against sunlight and apply calamine lotion or cool the skin with a damp cloth.

Prickly heat

This uncomfortable skin irritation can happen when excessive sweating blocks sweat pores. Remove any clothing, wash the affected skin in cool water, and put on dry clothes.

First aid kit

For any expedition, make sure you pack a first aid kit including painkillers, plasters, bandages, medical tape, scissors, bite and sting cream, insect repellent, tweezers, latex gloves, and any medication that specific expedition members may need, such as EpiPens or asthma inhalers.

Sterilizing wounds

Infection can set in fast in hot weather. Be sure to sterilize any wounds by washing carefully and applying antiseptic cream.

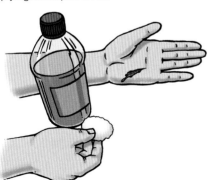

BEAR SAYS

Drink plenty of fluids in summer to avoid dehydration. If you become dehydrated, take small sips of water and rest in a cool place.

SUMMER HIKING

Summer is one of the best seasons to go hiking. Long hours of daylight allow for lengthy walks, but beware the sun around midday. The tips on this page will help you get the most out of a hiking trip.

Hiking kit
Don't forget these important items of kit on a hiking trip.

hiking boots

healthy, high-energy snacks

warm socks

compass

emergency blanket

waterproof jacket

sun hat

warm layers

Footwear
A sturdy pair of walking boots is invaluable on any hike. In dry conditions, walking shoes will also work well and are slightly cooler than boots.

Blisters
When it comes to blisters, prevention is better than a cure. Smear petroleum jelly between the toes to prevent rubbing. Take action as soon as you notice soreness. Remove boots and socks and apply a plaster or moleskin to protect the sore spot. If you do get a blister, don't pop it, or you will risk infection.

Walking stick

A good walking pole will provide extra stability. You can also use it to test the depth of streams or marshes, and keep brambles, nettles, and any curious animals at bay.

BEAR SAYS

Tell someone where you are going and what time you expect to reach your destination, so they can raise the alarm if you don't appear.

Climbing and descending

It's better to climb slowly and steadily rather than rushing, then having to stop to catch your breath. Zigzag up and down steep slopes. Tighten your boots before descending. Keep knees bent and use your stick to take your weight.

River crossings

Scout along the bank for the best place to cross, such as a shallow place or stepping stones. Undo the waist strap of your rucksack. Use your stick for stability. If in a group, link arms or hold onto rucksack straps.

NAVIGATION

Knowing how to read a map is vital both for short hikes or a major expedition. You should also carry a compass and know how to use it. With a map and compass you can find your way any time, anywhere!

Map symbols

Maps are drawings of the landscape from above. Features such as water, trees, tracks, and buildings are shown using symbols. The key, or legend, at the side explains what the symbols mean. On most maps, north is at the top.

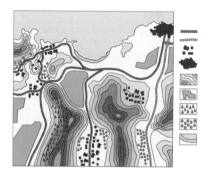

Contour lines

Contour lines show hills and valleys on the flat surface of a map. These lines link places at the same height above sea level. The height is also given in small figures. Check the figures to see if the land slopes up or down. Allow more time to climb steep hills.

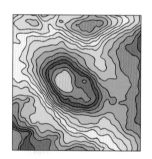

Grid references

Most maps are divided into a grid of squares. Each square is numbered, which allows you to find locations. Grid references give the east-west position first, then the north-south position. Counting the grid lines crossed on your route provides a rough idea of distance.

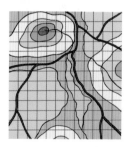

Scale

Everything on a map is drawn to the same size, called the scale. The scale bar in the key will help you to estimate how long a journey will take.

1 cm = 1 km

Compass

The red magnetic needle on a compass always points north. Hold the compass flat so the needle rotates freely, and keep it away from any metal objects, which could distort the reading.

BEAR SAYS

If you get lost, keep calm and look around. Can you spot any landmarks, such as a stream or path junction? See if you can spot that landmark on your map. If you have no idea where you are, look for a stream, follow it downhill until you find signs of civilization.

Using a map and compass

1. Rotate the inner dial so the red arrow points north on the map. The lines on the dial lie over the gridlines on the map.
2. Turn your body so the red magnetic arrow hovers over the red arrow. Now the features you see around you will relate to what's shown on the map.

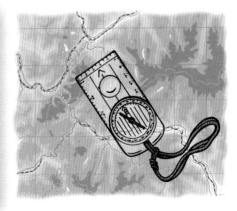

Navigating without a compass

Using a compass is the easiest way to navigate in the wild. It allows you to get your bearings, so you know which way to head. However, it is still possible to work out your direction if you don't have a compass.

Using a sun stick

Use this method on a sunny day to find the four main compass points: north, south, east, and west.

1. Push a long, straight stick into the ground. Mark the tip of the stick's shadow with a stone or twig.
2. Wait at least 15 minutes – an hour or more, if possible. The shadow will have moved round. Mark the new position with a second marker.
3. Draw a line between the two markers. This is your east-west line. Draw a second line at right-angles to the first – this is your north-south line.

1.

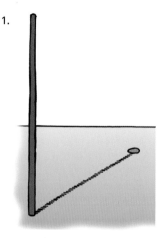

2.

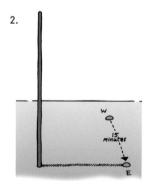

3.

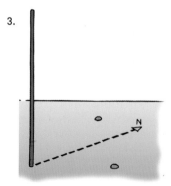

Using a wristwatch

This method is different in the northern and southern hemispheres. Hold your watch flat. In the northern hemisphere, point the hour hand at the sun. A line midway between the hour and 12 o'clock on your watch points due south. In the southern hemisphere, point 12 o'clock on your watch at the sun. A line midway between this and the hour hand points due north.

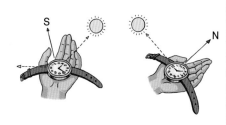

Navigating by the stars

In the northern hemisphere, the tip of the Plough (Big Dipper) points to the bright North Star, due north. In the southern hemisphere, the base of the Southern Cross (near a dark, starless patch called the Coal Sack) points south.

the Plough

the Southern Cross

Making a DIY compass

Improvize a compass using a needle and small bar magnet. Stroke the magnet along the length of the needle in one direction. Repeat many times. Place the magnetized needle on a leaf, bark, or paper, and float in water. It will settle to point north-south. Use the general direction of the sun to work out which is north.

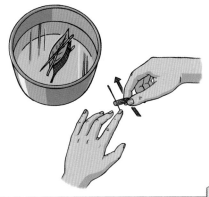

SIGNS AND SIGNALS

Signalling is an important skill. It allows you to communicate with others, mark a trail, and raise the alarm in an emergency. Summer is a great time to practise signalling, as it is likely to be sunny and dry. You will need basic equipment: a torch, a whistle, and a small mirror.

Types of signal
There are two main types of signal – visual (sight) and audio (sound) signals. These relate to our main senses, sight and hearing.

Trail signs
Scouts invented trail signs to mark the route for others to follow. You can use sticks, stones, or even tufts of grass to mark a trail.

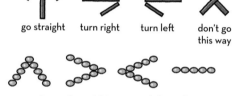

go straight   turn right   turn left   don't go this way

go straight   turn right   turn left   don't go this way

go straight   turn right   turn left   don't go this way   gone home

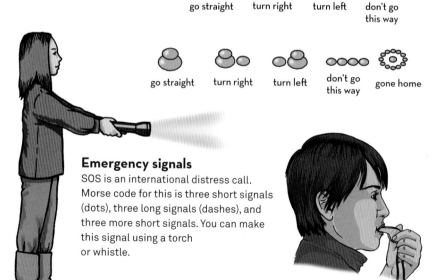

Emergency signals
SOS is an international distress call. Morse code for this is three short signals (dots), three long signals (dashes), and three more short signals. You can make this signal using a torch or whistle.

Signalling with a mirror

A flash of light from a mirror can be seen from far away. You can signal to your group or to an aircraft in an emergency. Hold the mirror at shoulder height and point towards the sun. Stretch out your other arm and spread your fingers. Now angle the mirror so reflected light passes between your fingers onto the target.

Body signals

Body signals can be used to communicate with aircraft in an emergency. Position yourself in the open and give signals very clearly.

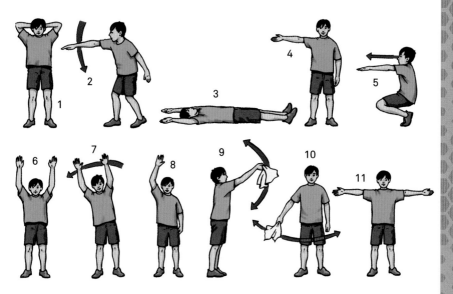

Key

1. Our receiver is operating
2. Use drop message
3. Need medical assistance
4. Wait, I can proceed shortly
5. Land here
6. Pick us up
7. Do not attempt to land here
8. All OK, do not wait
9. Yes
10. No
11. Need mechanical help

SUMMER CAMPING

Warm weather and light evenings make summer the best time for camping. The right gear will help you stay warm and comfortable overnight in the wild.

Choosing a tent

Tents come in different shapes and sizes. Practise putting up and taking down a new tent before a camping trip.

Sleeping bags

These are generally graded by season – in most places, you will only need a light bag for summer. Bags filled with man-made fibre are relatively cheap and effective even if wet. You can also buy down-filled bags, but these are very warm and ineffective when wet, so are most likely inappropriate for summer camping.

Mattresses

Camping mats and mattresses provide comfort and insulation from damp ground. A foam mat is light to carry. In a survival situation, you could make a bough bed (see pages 22–23).

Camping kit

These items will come in handy when camping.

rope

torch

ground sheet

tarpaulin

insect repellent candle

portable shower

foot pump

towel

Cooking kit

You'll need pots, pans, and other utensils if you intend to cook in the wild.

chopping board

camping mug

cutlery

sharp knife

tea towel

pan

wooden spoon

drinking water

Stoves

Camping stoves provide instant heat that is easy to control. Various designs run on gas, petrol, or solid fuel. Don't forget to take spare fuel. You can also cook on a campfire or with charcoal on a barbecue.

BEAR SAYS

Plan camp menus in advance, and make a list of all the ingredients you need. You don't want to start cooking only to discover that a vital ingredient is missing!

Making camp

Your camp is a home from home. It's a place to sleep, eat, bond with friends, and get close to nature. The right location and good organization will help your camp run more efficiently.

Campsite location

Site your camp near a source of wood and water. Don't pitch too close to water, though, or you risk getting flooded or eaten by mosquitoes! The best sites are sheltered yet sunny. Beware rotten trees or branches that could fall and hurt you or damage your equipment. Also beware ant, wasp, and bee nests.

BEAR SAYS

Don't leave tools and kit lying around, as they could get wet or rusty. Choose a place to keep equipment, and ask everyone to return things after use.

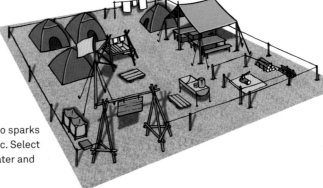

Camp layout

Build your campfire downwind of tents so sparks can't ignite the fabric. Select a place to collect water and don't wash there.

Pitching tents

Choose flattish ground and remove debris. Hammer pegs in firmly, trying not to bend them. Pull guy-ropes taut to keep the tent from being blown down if it gets windy.

Timber hitch

This is a good knot for attaching cord to posts or saplings. Loop one end around the post and then over the standing cord. Thread the end below the cord over the post several times. Tighten by pulling the standing cord.

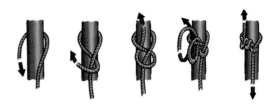

Food cache

Keep food in tightly sealed containers. In bear country, you will need to cache food high in the air. Tie the bag onto a rope and throw the rope over a high branch and hoist into the air.

Ticks and insects

Mosquitoes can carry dangerous diseases. Apply jungle-strength repellent and keep your skin covered. Sleep under a mosquito net. Beware ticks in woods and on farmland. If one gets stuck in your skin, use tweezers to seize the body, wait a split-second, then pull gently, so the head comes out too.

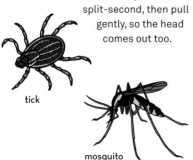

tick

mosquito

EMERGENCY SHELTERS

A shelter protects you from the elements. It helps you to get a good night's sleep, so you can be alert the next day. Summer is a great time to practise building shelters with rope and tarpaulin, or just using natural materials around you.

Tarp shelters

With rope and a tarp or plastic sheet, you can quickly rig a basic shelter to keep the rain off. There are several different designs. Make sure the entrance to your shelter faces away from the wind.

Tepee shelter

Gather several stout sticks and create a tepee shape, lashing the sticks together at the top and spreading the legs to create a sturdy structure. Cover this structure with a tarp, securing at the bottom with stones.

Fold-over shelter

Drive two stout branches into the ground. Secure with guy-ropes if needed. Tie a cord between the uprights and pull taut. Throw a tarp over, attach cords, and peg it down. Fold the excess material under to make a groundsheet.

Building a forest lean-to

1. Lash a long, straightish branch between two uprights at around waist-height to form a ridgepole. Peg logs to form the base of the shelter.
2. Lash 4–5 straightish branches sloping from the ridgepole to the base. Weave lots of smaller, supple, leafy branches between these to form a roof. Start at the bottom and work up.
3. If desired, drive shorter branches into the ground at the sides, and weave in twigs to form walls.

Bivouac in the open

A bivvy bag is a large, waterproof bag that provides emergency shelter. You may be able to pile rocks to form walls for a windbreak.

Making a bough bed

Dry leaves, bracken, and grass can be used as bedding. You can also pile spruce or pine branches inside a bed-shaped frame of branches pegged to the ground.

FINDING WATER AND FOOD

Drinking enough fluid is more important than eating, particularly in hot weather. You need to drink several litres of water a day to replace fluids lost naturally. Purify water from rivers, lakes, and streams.

Collecting water

Collect water from the surface of fast-flowing streams and rivers if possible, as it will be cleaner. Wade out into a lake to collect water at the surface. Never use a source that looks polluted. Freshly collected rainwater should be pure enough to drink – place containers to catch runoff from tents or roofs.

Gathering dew

Dew condenses on cold surfaces at dusk and dawn. Mop dew from your tent with a clean cloth or sponge, then wring the moisture into a container. You can also gather water by tying cloths to your ankles and walking through dew-soaked grass.

Using a transpiration bag

Place a plastic bag over a leafy branch in the sun. Tie the neck securely. Water given off by the leaves will condense and trickle down inside the bag.

Edible plants

Blackberries, bilberries, wild raspberries, and strawberries are delicious. Rosehips and crab apples are better stewed. Hazelnuts and sweet chestnuts (not conkers) can be roasted. Young, tender leaves of dock, chickweed, and plantain are edible when cooked.

blackberry

wild raspberry

strawberry

hazelnut

crab apples

plantain

sweet chestnut

bilberry

dock leaf

rosehips

chickweed

Edible fungi

Field and parasol mushrooms are edible when cooked. So are oyster and beefsteak fungus, which grow on trees. You must be 100 per cent sure you have identified fungi correctly before eating.

field mushroom

parasol mushroom

beefsteak fungus

oyster fungus

BEAR SAYS

All water except fresh rainwater must be purified before drinking. You can use a sock to filter debris. Boil water for at least five minutes to kill germs, or use purification tablets.

Poisonous fungi

Many fungi are highly poisonous. Beware destroying angel, deathcap, and fly agaric. Don't take a chance with fungi – if in doubt, leave it out.

death cap

fly agaric

destroying angel

GOING FISHING

Rivers, lakes, and coastal waters contain fish, which are a valuable source of protein. Pretty much all freshwater fish are edible. They are probably the easiest game to catch in a survival situation, but you have to be patient.

DIY fishing tackle

Rig fishing tackle with nylon line and a hook or safety pin. Attach a stick so you can cast away from the bank. Improvize a weight and float. Bait your line with a worm or fish guts – and happy hunting!

Improvizing a fishing spear

Make a cross-shaped cut in the end of a stout stick or bamboo. The cuts should extend about 15 cm down the shaft. Bind the stick behind the cuts to prevent splitting. Loop string around to separate the prongs, and carve sharp points.

Spear fishing

Stand on a rock with your spear tip poised just above the surface. Experiment with your aim, as the water's reflection may warp the size and position of the fish. When a fish comes into range, strike to pin the fish to the bottom.

Making a bottle trap

Cut off the top of a plastic bottle. Insert bait and wedge the top upside-down inside the base. Wedge securely among rocks on the bottom. Fish entering to take the bait won't be able to escape.

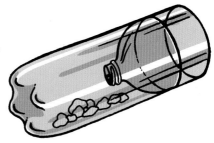

How to make a fishing weir

Drive sticks into the stream bed to form a trap facing upstream. The sticks must be close together. Use more sticks to create a funnel to direct fish into the trap.

BEAR SAYS

In hot weather, fish lurk in the shadows below banks and bridges. Dusk and dawn are the best times to hunt.

Gutting a fish

Fish more than 5 cm long must be gutted before cooking. Remove the head, gills, and tail. Slit the underside and remove the insides with your knife.

WILDLIFE WATCHING

Patience is essential if you want to observe wild animals. You've got to be still and quiet to have any chance of getting close to wary creatures. For this reason, warm summer days and evenings are ideal for wildlife watching.

Tracks
Animals can be identified from the prints they leave in mud or sand. A field guide to local wildlife will show tracks made by animals in your area. Find out when animals are active.

Trails and traces
Foxes, deer, and other wildlife wear narrow trails as they forage for food or patrol the borders of their territory. You can also look for food remains such as nibbled shoots, bark, or nuts.

BEAR SAYS

Move slowly and stealthily, keeping to cover where possible. Avoid treading on dry twigs or leaves. If spotted, keep absolutely still until the animal relaxes again.

Camouflage

Wear dull-coloured clothing that blends in with the background to go wildlife watching. You can smear mud to disguise exposed skin such as your face and hands. Leafy twigs stuck in your hat will help disguise your outline.

Using cover

Often the most effective method is to sit still and let animals approach you. Make as little noise as possible and avoid sudden movements. Hide behind cover such as bushes, trees, or long grass, sit tight, and be prepared to wait.

Approach downwind

If you approach animals upwind, the breeze will carry your scent and give you away. Test wind direction by holding up a wet finger, or watch foliage moving. Circle to get downwind of animals.

Leopard crawl

Move forward on all fours, with your weight on knees and elbows. Move your right arm and left leg together, then the opposite pair.

MAKING A CAMPFIRE

In summer, you may not need a fire for warmth, but you'll need one to cook and boil water. Fire also provides a means of drying clothes and keeping insects and wild animals at bay.

Science of fire

Fire requires three things: heat, fuel, and oxygen. Remove any one of these and the fire goes out. Use this science to control your fire. For example, smother a fire with earth to remove oxygen if you want it to go out, or add fuel if you want the fire to burn more strongly.

Gathering fuel

Begin by gathering fuel. You will need dry tinder such as grasses, birch bark, or wood shavings, kindling (small sticks), and then small and larger logs.

Building a tepee fire

A pyramid-shaped tepee fire is easy to light. Make a small pile of tinder, then build kindling in a pyramid above it. A ring of stones or two large logs can be used to contain the fire.

Fire-lighting
The easiest way to light a fire is using matches or a lighter. Use your body as a windshield and cup your hands around the flame. Hold a lighted match sloping downwards. Never strike a match towards yourself.

Using a fire steel
A fire steel creates sparks to ignite tinder. Hold the steel just above the tinder with the striker over it. Draw the striker back against the steel to direct sparks onto the tinder.

BEAR SAYS
Fires are particularly dangerous in hot, dry weather. Stray sparks could easily start a forest fire. Beware of drifting sparks, and have water standing by to douse the flames if needed.

Using a magnifying glass
In direct sunlight, angle a magnifying glass so light passes through the lens onto the tinder. Smoke will start to rise, then the tinder will ignite.

CAMP COOKING

Nothing tastes better than food cooked on a campfire after a long day outdoors. You can cook in different ways using a stove, barbecue, or campfire – food can be grilled, stewed, fried, roasted, or baked in the embers of your fire.

Spit roasting
Drive two strong, forked sticks into the ground on either side of the fire. Point one end of a strong, green (freshly cut) stick and skewer your meat or fish. Place on the spit and turn occasionally so the food cooks evenly.

Stewing and boiling
Large, flat stones form a firm base for a saucepan in which you can cook a stew.

Grilling
Skewers of meat, fish, fruit, or vegetables can be grilled on a barbecue or campfire.

Making a tripod

A tripod is useful for heating food and boiling water. You need three long, strong, straightish sticks. Bind tightly at one end, then splay the other ends to form the tripod. Suspend a pan or kettle above the fire on a pot hanger (see pages 34–35).

Using a drying rack

The tripod design can also be used to make a drying rack. Bind three sticks to the struts, and use green, supple twigs to weave a mesh between them. Place thin strips of food on the rack and light a small, smoky fire beneath.

Making a pot rod

Cut a notch near the end of a strong, freshly cut stick. Wedge it under rocks and over a large log or forked stick to suspend a pot above a fire.

Baking in foil

Fish, game, potatoes, or fruit can be cooked in foil in the embers of a campfire or barbecue. Wrap the food in foil to create an airtight package. Use tongs to place in the embers, turn, and remove when cooked.

BUSHCRAFT

Bushcraft is the art of making yourself at home in the wild. With a few simple tools and a little skill you can make all sorts of useful objects that will make camp life more comfortable.

Making cordage

Cordage is rope, string, or cord. You can make cordage from tough plant fibres such as reeds and vines. You can also use nettles, but crush them first to neutralize the stinging hairs. Roll the fibres between your palms and tie a knot at one end. Join two strands by plaiting or rolling in the opposite direction.

Tying a reef knot

A reef knot is a very versatile knot. Pass the right end over, then under, the left end. Now pass the left end over and then under the right. Tighten by pulling the two ends.

Tying an overhand knot

Tie an overhand loop to form a fixed loop in a rope. Loop the rope over itself and then pull the loop through the hole.

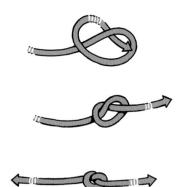

Carving a wooden spoon

A hand-carved spoon is a simple craft that provides a lasting memento of time spent in the wild.

1. Find a dry piece of wood about 25 cm long, 5–7 cm wide, and 3–4 cm thick. You can also cut and split a larger piece using a saw and hand axe.
2. Use a knife to shape the handle and the back of the bowl. Now trim the sides of the bowl into an oval shape.
3. Hollow out the bowl using a gouging tool or the curved end of your knife. Smooth with a knife or sandpaper.

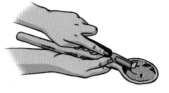

Make pot hangers

Pot hangers can be made from forked sticks. Trim the forks to make hooks. Alternatively, you can carve a hook in a straight stick by cutting a neat X-shape with your knife. Pare away the wood from three-quarters of the X. Deepen the notch if required.

CAMPFIRE SURVIVAL STORIES

The fire is the heart of any camp. It's a great place to get together and swap stories. Survival tales can provide useful safety tips, and also inspiration for your own adventures.

Lost in the jungle

In 2007, two men got lost on a 125-km hike through the Amazon. After running out of food, they survived by eating palm seeds, grubs, and centipedes. They also ate poisonous spiders after cooking them to neutralize the poison. Eventually, after seven weeks in the wild, they made it out alive.

Island survivor

During World War II, Japanese solider Shoichi Yokoi was posted on a remote Pacific island. He fled into the jungle when enemy troops arrived. Yokoi lived on fruit, snails, fish, and coconuts. He lived in an underground cave, which he dug using a handmade trowel. After an incredible 28 years, he was found, and learned World War II was long over.

Trapped in a canyon

In 2003, a young hiker was walking in a deep canyon in Utah, USA, when a boulder slipped and trapped his hand. After six days, facing starvation, he cut off his own hand using a multi-tool and limped to safety.

Head downstream

In 1971, a teenager was stranded in the Amazon after her plane crashed. Alone, she remembered her father's advice to head downstream if you are lost – eventually, you are likely to reach civilization. After nine days, Juliane reached the safety of a hunter's camp, where she dug 50 maggots out of her skin!

Fluid in the desert

In 1994, an Italian marathon runner got lost in the Sahara Desert during a sandstorm. He survived by drinking his own urine and eating bats and reptiles. After nine days, he finally reached the safety of an oasis.

ON THE WATER

Summer is the best season to go boating, whether in a canoe, dinghy, raft, or rowing boat. The tips on this page will help you stay afloat, and know what to do if you capsize.

Clothing and equipment

Wear windproof or waterproof clothing, and deck shoes or plastic sandals. Vital safety gear should include a lifejacket and helmet for white water. Take rope, a container to bail with, and dry clothes in a sealed plastic bag.

helmet

lifejacket

rope

suncream

plastic bags

bucket

deck shoes

waterproof jacket

Preparation

Before you set off, check tide times and wind speeds and direction. Check the forecast for hazards such as fog, mist, and squalls.

DOs and DON'Ts

DO wear a life jacket.

DO be courteous to other water users.

DON'T overload your craft with gear or people. Stow all gear securely.

DON'T ignore a bad weather forecast or problems such as leaks.

Kayak capsize

A technique called an eskimo roll rights a kayak that has overturned. You use the paddle as a lever and twist your hips to flip the boat upright. It takes skill and practice. If you haven't mastered this trick, practise exiting an overturned kayak by lifting the spray deck, grabbing the rim, and pushing yourself out.

Righting a dinghy

Brace your feet against the hull and pull on a rope or the dagger board. Walk over the hull as the craft rights itself. If you can't right your vessel, stay with it, as you will be much easier to spot.

In the water

If your boat sinks in open water, don't exhaust yourself swimming. Just stay afloat by treading water. Keep your body upright and move your arms and legs in small circles. If wearing a life jacket, conserve body heat by crossing your arms and legs.

BEAR SAYS

If canoeing or boating in rough seas, keep your craft pointed into the waves. Even a small wave could capsize you if it hits your boat side-on.

BUILDING A RAFT

Rafts are one of the very oldest forms of water transport. With rope and some timber, you can practise the ancient art of raft-building. In a survival situation, you can use a raft to escape from dense jungle or a desert island.

Building a driftwood raft

1. Scout along the shore for materials such as driftwood, rope, netting, and floats. Lash long timbers together with rope to form the base of the raft. Tie all knots tightly.
2. Lash more timbers at right-angles to the first layer. If you have an axe, cut notches in the base for these cross-struts.
3. Test the raft for buoyancy. Floating objects can be lashed to the underside to improve buoyancy.
4. Rafts are hard to steer. Use a plank for a rudder – lash it to an A-frame near the stern.
5. If desired, you can raise a mast and add canvas, plastic sheeting, or woven leaves to provide shade and a sail.
6. Use spare timber to make a paddle. In shallow water, you can punt with a pole.

Bamboo raft

Bamboo is an excellent material for raft-building. Cut poles about 3 m long, using a machete. Use the point of a knife to make two lines of holes through the poles. Thread rope or thin canes through the holes to lash the raft together. Add a second layer of poles.

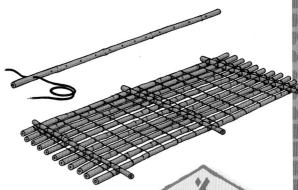

Before launching

Check winds, waves, tides, and currents before launching. If you have a map, scan for hazards such as reefs, shoals, and rapids. On a river, watch for overhanging branches. Listen for the sound of crashing water, which could indicate a waterfall ahead.

BEAR SAYS

Build your raft close to the water's edge so it can be launched easily, but beware changing water levels due to rainfall or tides.

WILD SWIMMING

Swimming in places such as lakes, rivers, and the seashore is known as wild swimming. Warm air and water temperatures make summer the best time for swimming. Knowing how to swim strongly and safely is a vital survival skill.

Swimwear and kit

A wetsuit, gloves, and swim hat may be needed for long-distance and cold-water swimming. Goggles and a whistle will come in handy. Plastic shoes make it easier to enter and leave the water. Don't forget your towel!

towel

goggles

swim hat

whistle

gloves

plastic shoes

wetsuit

DOs and DON'Ts

DO keep track of your position in the sea or a river. Notice which way you are drifting and don't get swept away.

DO watch for overhanging branches that could pull you under in a swift current.

DON'T swim alone or at night.
DON'T dive off rocks into water of uncertain depth.

Preparation

As for boating, check currents and tides, wind speeds, and direction. Don't swim in stormy weather. Beware steep banks and thick mud along rivers. Weeds and other floating objects show where the current is flowing fast.

Offshore currents

If you are swept offshore by a current, don't try to swim directly against it. Swim diagonally to shore, or float along the coast until the current slackens, then make for land.

Swimming in surf

Strong surf can create a powerful undertow. Face the waves. Dive under breakers and surface once the wave has passed. Beware of reefs and rocks.

BEAR SAYS

Don't swim close to boats with outboard motors. Whirling propellers are very dangerous. Give all craft a wide berth, and make sure other water users have seen you.

Escaping from a whirlpool

Whirlpools can form below weirs and dams, or where currents meet offshore. If caught in a whirlpool, don't panic. If you go with the flow, the current may slacken. Or take a deep breath and dive down – the current may weaken or throw you out.

ON THE BEACH

For many people, summer means going to the beach. In a survival situation, beaches are great places to find food and rig a shelter. However, tides, currents, and some sea creatures can be dangerous, so it always pays to take care.

Tides and currents

Water levels on many beaches change dramatically as tides rise and fall. Tides can also create strong offshore currents. Find out what the tide is doing. Don't get cut off by a rising tide.

Foraging

Seashores contain abundant food if you know where to look for it. Hunt for fish, shrimps, and crabs in rockpools, and prize limpets off rocks using a penknife. Seaweeds such as kelp and sea lettuce taste great in a seafood casserole.

Cracking a coconut

Coconuts are a valuable food source. Ram the eye onto a sharpened stake. Drink the fluid, then crack the nut open and eat the flesh.

Beachcombing
In a survival situation, check along the tideline for useful debris such as bottles, containers, nets, and floats – and, of course, driftwood to build a fire.

Caves
Caves can offer shelter on a beach but, before moving in, you have to be absolutely sure the cave won't fill with water at high tide. Check the cave walls for signs of rising tides and damp.

Rigging a beach shelter
Site your shelter above the high tide mark. Make an A-frame by lashing wooden spars together. Push the ends into the sand. Tie on a ridgepole sloping downwards, then lay sticks vertically against the ridgepole. Use thorns or string to secure large leaves to form a thatch.

BEAR SAYS
Beware of jellyfish. Most jellyfish stings are painful but not dangerous, but the sting of a box jellyfish can be fatal.

GLOSSARY

Antiseptic – Something that prevents infection by killing germs.

Audio – Relating to sound.

Bearing – The direction in which you are headed, as shown on a compass.

Buoyancy – Ability to float.

Bushcraft – Survival skills used in the wild.

Cache – A hidden store, or to hide something.

Capsize – When a boat overturns.

Cordage – Rope, string, or cord.

Condense – When water changes from a gas into a liquid.

Contour lines – Lines on a map joining places at the same height.

Cumulonimbus – A tall, dark, flat-topped thundercloud.

Debris – Pieces of waste material.

Dehydration – When the body lacks water.

Evaporation – When water changes from a liquid into a gas.

Forage – To obtain food from the wild.

Grid reference – Numbers referring to the grid squares on a map and used to pinpoint locations.

Hemisphere – One half of the Earth, as divided by the Equator.

Hull – The body of a ship or boat.

Ignite – To set light to something.

Insulate – To keep something warm.

Isobars – Lines on a weather map joining areas of equal air pressure.

Protein – Nutrient found in meat, fish, milk, eggs, nuts, and beans.

Ridgepole – The long, horizontal pole of a tent which supports the fabric.

Rudder – The steering mechanism on a boat.

Scale – The size a map is drawn to.

Squall – A sudden, violent gust of wind, which may bring rain.

Tarpaulin – Thick waterproof cloth, usually with eyeholes in the corners for attaching. Often called a tarp.

Transpiration – Process by which a plant gives off excess moisture through its leaves.

Utensil – A tool or container, usually used in cooking.

Visual – Relating to sight.

Discover more amazing books in the Bear Grylls series:

Perfect for young adventurers, the *Survival Skills* series accompanies an exciting range of colouring and activity books. Curious kids can also learn tips and tricks for almost any extreme situation in *Survival Camp*, explore Earth in *Extreme Planet*, and discover some of history's greatest explorers in the *Epic Adventures* series.

Conceived by Bonnier Books UK
in partnership with Bear Grylls Ventures

Produced by Bonnier Books UK
Suite 3.08 The Plaza, 535 Kings Road,
London SW10 0SZ, UK

BONNIER BOOKS UK
Editor Susie Rae
Designer Shahid Mahmood
Contributor Jen Green
Illustrator Julian Baker

Disclaimer

Bonnier Books UK and Bear Grylls take pride in doing our best to get the facts right in putting together the information in this book, but occasionally something slips past our beady eyes. Therefore we make no warranties about the accuracy or completeness of the information in the book and to the maximum extent permitted, we disclaim all liability. Wherever possible, we will endeavour to correct any errors of fact at reprint.

Kids – if you want to try any of the activities in this book, please ask your parents first! Parents – all outdoor activities carry some degree of risk and we recommend that anyone participating in these activities be aware of the risks involved and seek professional instruction and guidance. None of the health/medical information in this book is intended as a substitute for professional medical advice; always seek the advice of a qualified practitioner.